NEET BIOLOGY NOTES

ANIMAL KINGDOM

BY

Dr Javid Ahmad

KINGDOM ANIMALIA

This kingdom is of heterotrophic eukaryotic organisms. They are **multicellular** and their cells lack cell walls. They directly or indirectly depend on plants for food. They digest their food in an internal cavity and store food reserves as **glycogen** or **fat**. Their mode of nutrition is **holozoic** – by ingestion of food. They follow a definite growth pattern and grow into adults that have a definite shape and size. Higher forms show elaborate sensory and neuromotor mechanism. Most of them are capable of **locomotion**. The sexual reproduction is by copulation of male and female followed by embryological development.

1. Basis for classification

In spite of the differences in structure and form of different animals, there are fundamental features common to various individuals in relation to:

    (a) the arrangement of cells,

    (b) body symmetry,

    (c)   nature of coelom,

    (d)   patterns of digestive, circulatory or reproductive systems.

These features are used as the basis of animal classification and some of them are discussed here.

(I) Levels of Organisation

Though all members of Animalia are **multicellular**, all of them do not exhibit the same pattern of organisation of cells. Different levels of organisation are:

    i.   <u>**Cellular level:**</u> The cells are arranged as loose cell aggregates. For example in **sponges.** Some division of labour (activities) occur among the cells.

ii. **Tissue level:** In **coelenterates**, the arrangement of cells is more complex. Here the cells performing the same function are arranged into tissues.

iii. **Organ level:** A still higher level of organisation, i.e., ***organ level*** is exhibited by members of **Platyhelminthes** and other higher phyla where tissues are grouped together to form organs, each specialized for a particular function.

iv. **Organ system level:** In animals like **Annelids, Arthropods, Molluscs, Echinoderms** and **Chordates**, organs have associated to form functional systems, each system concerned with a specific physiological function. This pattern is called ***organ system*** level of organisation. Organ systems in different groups of animals exhibit various patterns of complexities. For example, the digestive system in Platyhelminthes has only a single opening to the outside of the body that serves as both mouth and anus, and is hence called **incomplete**. A **complete** digestive system has two openings, mouth and anus. Similarly, the circulatory system may be of two types: **Open type** in which the blood is pumped out of the heart and the cells and tissues are directly bathed in it and **Closed type** in which the blood is circulated through a series of vessels of varying diameters (arteries, veins and capillaries).

(II) Symmetry

Animals can be categorised on the basis of their symmetry as:

i. **Asymmetrical**: Sponges are mostly *asymmetrical,* i.e., any plane that passes through the centre does not divide them into equal halves.

ii. **Radial symmetry***:* When any plane passing through the central axis of the body divides the organism into two identical halves, it is called *radial symmetry*. Coelenterates, ctenophores and echinoderms have this kind of body plan (**Fig.1a**).

iii. **Bilateral symmetry***:* Animals like annelids, arthropods, etc., where the body can be divided into identical left and right halves in only one plane, exhibit *bilateral symmetry* **Fig.1b**).

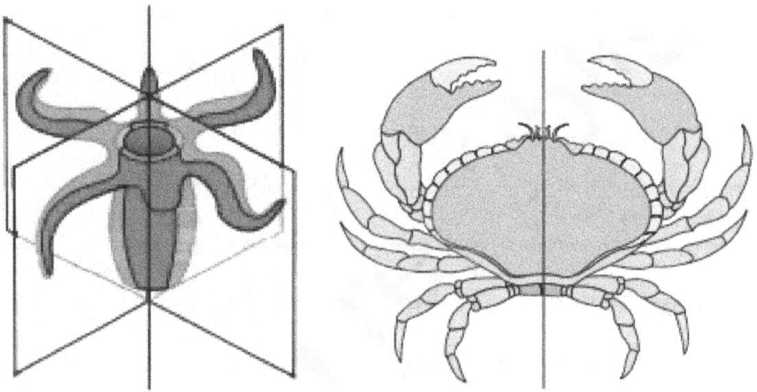

Fig.1 (a) *Radial symmetry* (b) *Bilateral symmetry*

(III) Diploblastic and Triploblastic Organisation

(i) **Diploblastic**: Animals in which the cells are arranged in two embryonic layers, an external *ectoderm* and an internal *endoderm*, are called *diploblastic* animals, e.g., coelenterates. An undifferentiated layer, *mesoglea*, is present in between the ectoderm and the endoderm (**Fig.2a**).

(ii) <u>**Triploblastic**</u>: Those animals in which the developing embryo has a third germinal layer, **mesoderm**, in between the ectoderm and endoderm, are called *triploblastic* animals (platyhelminthes to chordates, **Fig.2b**).

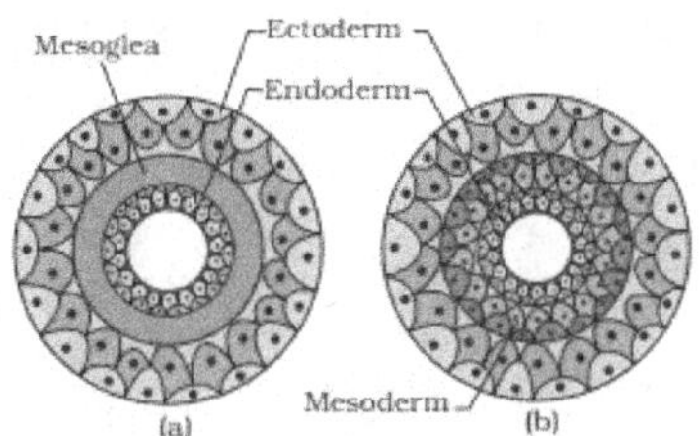

Fig 2. Showing germinal layers a) diploblastic b) triploblastic

(IV) Coelom

Presence or absence of a **cavity** between the body wall and the gut wall is very important in classification. The body cavity, which is lined by mesoderm is called **coelom**. Animals are of **three** types based on coelom organization:

i. <u>**Acoelomates**</u>: The animals in which the body cavity is absent are called **acoelomates,** e.g., platyhelminthes (**Fig.3c**).

ii. <u>**Pseudocoelomates**</u>*:* In some animals, the body cavity is not lined by mesoderm, instead, the mesoderm is present as scattered pouches in between the ectoderm and endoderm. Such a body cavity is called pseudocoelom and the animals possessing them are called **pseudocoelomates,** e.g., aschelminthes (**Fig.3b**).

iii. <u>**Coelomates**</u>*:* Animals possessing coelom are called **coelomates,** e.g., annelids, molluscs, arthropods, echinoderms, hemichordates and chordates (**Fig.3a**).

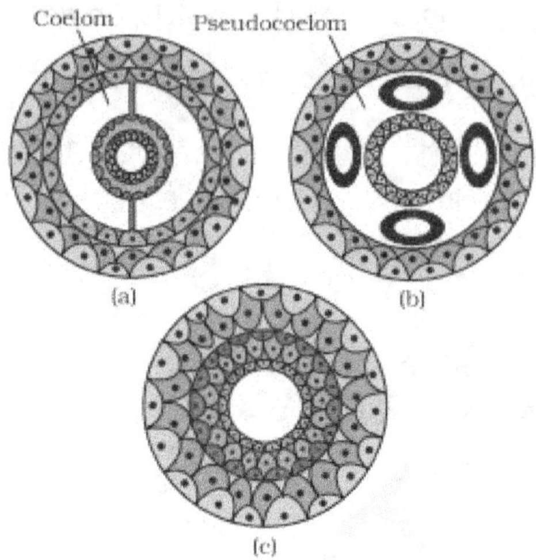

Fig.3 (a) ***Coelomate*** (b) ***Pseudocoelomates*** (C) ***Coelomates***

(V) Segmentation

In some animals, the body is externally and internally **divided into segments** with a **serial repetition** of at least some organs. For example, in earthworm, the body shows this pattern called metameric segmentation and the phenomenon is known as **metamerism.**

(VI) Notochord

Notochord is a **mesodermally** derived rod-like structure formed on the dorsal side during embryonic development in some animals.

   i.   **Chordates:** Animals with notochord at any stage of life are called **chordates.**

   ii.   **Non-chordates:** Animals which do not form notochord are called **non-chordates**, e.g., porifera to echinoderms.

2. CLASSIFICATION OF ANIMALS

The broad classification of Animalia based on common fundamental features as mentioned above is given in **Fig.4.**

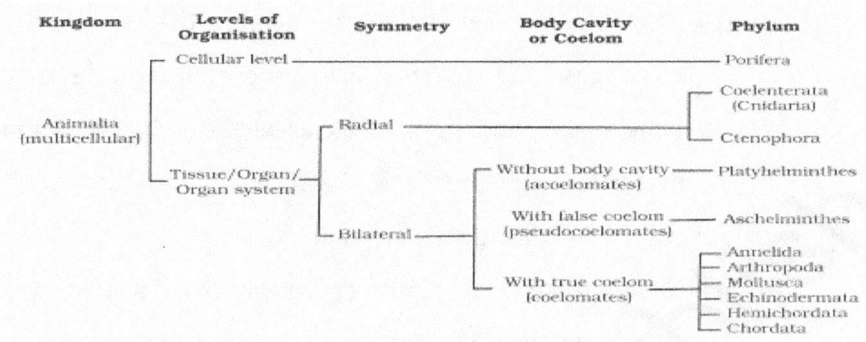

Fig.4. Broad classification of kingdom Animalia based on common *fundamental features*

The important characteristic features of the different phyla are described as follows:

(I) Phylum – Porifera (Sponges)

(i) **Habitat**: Aquatic, generally **marine**, some are freshwater (e.g., *Spongilla*)

(ii) **Symmetry**: Mostly **asymmetrical** animals (**Fig.5**).

(iii) **Organisation**: These are primitive multicellular animals and have **cellular** level of organisation.

(iv) **Canal system**: They have a water transport or **canal** system. Water enters through minute pores (**ostia**) in the body wall into a central cavity, **spongocoel**, from where it goes out through the **osculum**. This pathway of water transport is helpful in food gathering, respiratory exchange and removal of waste. **Choanocytes** or **collar cells** line the spongocoel and the canals.

(v) **Digestion** is **intracellular**.

(vi) **Skeleton**: The body is supported by a skeleton made up of **spicules** or **sponging fibres**.

(vii) **Reproduction**: Sexes are not separate (**hermaphrodite**), i.e., eggs and sperms are produced by the same individual. Sponges reproduce asexually by **fragmentation** and sexually by formation of **gametes**.

(viii) **Fertilisation** is **internal**.

(ix) **Development** is **indirect** having a larval stage (**amphiblastula, parenchymulla**) which is morphologically distinct from the adult.

(x) **Examples**: *Sycon* (Scypha), *Spongilla* (Fresh water sponge) and *Euspongia* (Bath sponge).

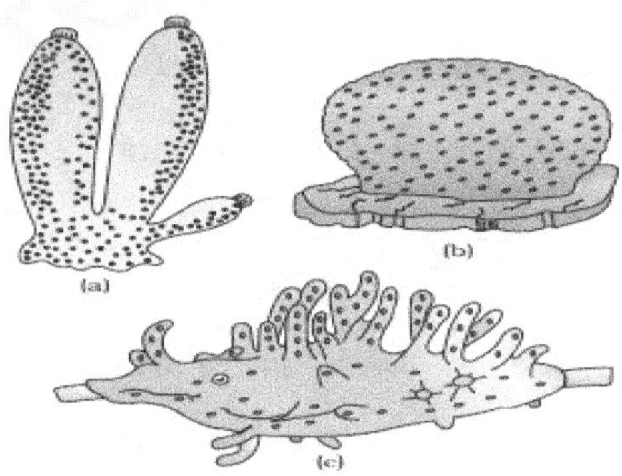

Fig 5. Examples of Porifera a) *Sycon* b) *Euspongia* c) *Spongilla*

(II) Phylum – Coelenterata (Cnidaria)

(i) **Habitat**: Aquatic, mostly marine, sessile or free-swimming.

(ii) **Symmetry**: Radially symmetrical animals (**Fig.6**).

(iii) **Cnidoblasts**: The name cnidaria is derived from the cnidoblast or cnidocytes (which contain the stinging capsules or nematocytes) present on the tentacles and the body. Cnidoblasts are used for anchorage, defense and for the capture of prey (**Fig.7**).

(iv) **Organisation**: Exhibit tissue level of organisation and are diploblastic.

(v) **Gastro-vascular cavity:**They have a central gastro-vascular cavity with a single opening, mouth on *hypostome*.

(vi) **Digestion** is extracellular and intracellular.

(vii)**Skeleton**: Some of the cnidarians, e.g., **corals** have a skeleton composed of **calcium carbonate**.

(viii) **Body forms**: Cnidarians exhibit two basic body forms called **polyp** and **medusa (Fig.6)**. **Polyp** is a sessile and cylindrical form like Hydra, *Adamsia*, etc. **Medusa** is umbrella-shaped and free-swimming like *Aurelia* or jelly fish.

(ix) **Metagenesis:** Those cnidarians which exist in both forms exhibit alternation of generation (**Metagenesis**), i.e., polyps produce medusae **asexually** and medusae form the polyps **sexually** (e.g., *Obelia*).

Examples: *Physalia* (Portuguese man-of-war), *Adamsia* (Sea anemone), *Pennatula* (Sea-pen), *Gorgonia* (Sea-fan) and *Meandrina* (Brain coral).

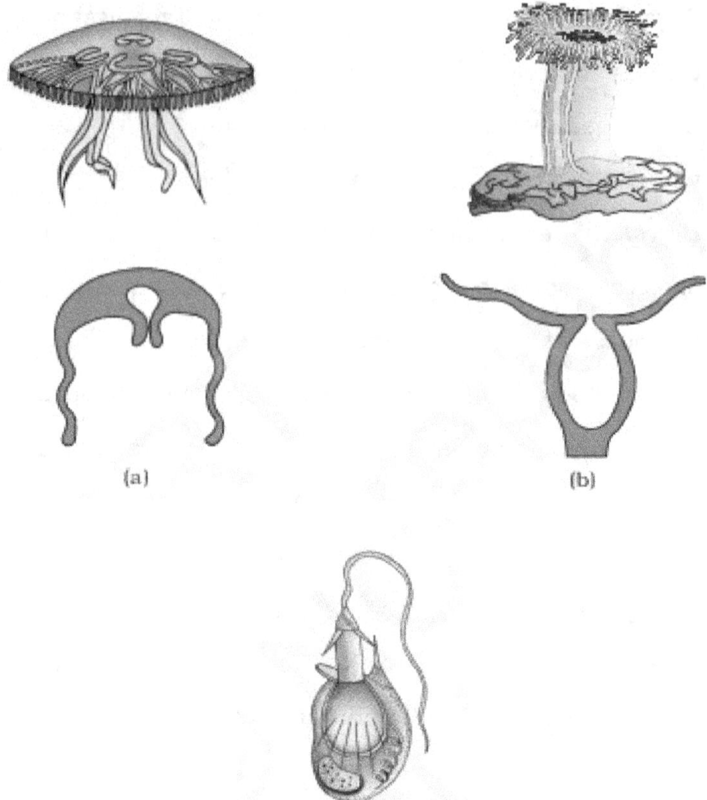

Fig 6.Examples of coelenterates (with outline of their body form) **Fig 7**.
Cnidoblast *Aurelia* –Medusa b) *Adamsia* -polyp

(III) Phylum – Ctenophora (Sea walnuts or Comb jellies)

(i)   **Habitat**: They are exclusively marine.

(ii) **Symmetry:** Radially symmetrical, diploblastic organisms with tissue level of organisation.

(iii) **Comb plates:** The body bears eight external rows of ciliated *comb plates*, which help in **locomotion (Fig.8)**.

(iv) **Digestion** is both extracellular and intracellular.

(v)   **Bioluminescence** (the property of a living organism to emit light) is well-marked in ctenophores.

(vi) **Reproduction:** Sexes are not separate. Reproduction takes place **only by sexual** means.

(vii) **Fertilisation** is **external** with **indirect** development.

Examples: *Pleurobrachia* and *Ctenoplana*.

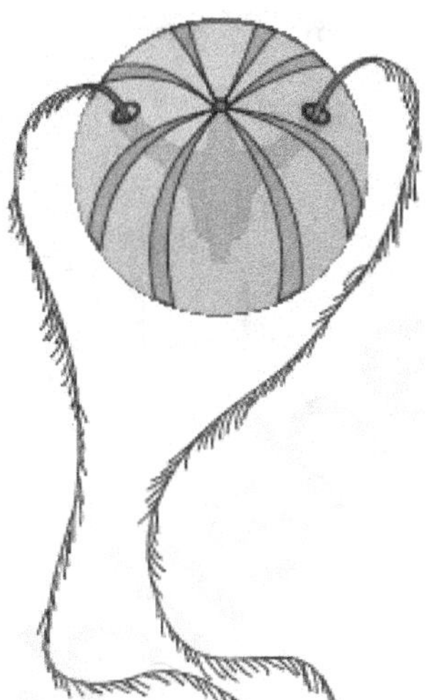

Fig. 8. *Pleurobrachia*

(IV) Phylum – Platyhelminthes (Flatworms)

(i) **Habitat**: These are mostly **endoparasites** found in animals including human beings. They have dorso-ventrally flattened body, hence are called **flatworms** (*Fig.*9).

(ii) **Symmetry:** Bilaterally symmetrical.

(iii) **Organisation: Triploblastic** and **acoelomate** animals with **organ level** of organisation.

(iv) **Hooks and suckers** are present in the parasitic forms.

(v) **Nutrition:** Some of them (**tapeworms-cestodes**) absorb nutrients from the host directly through their body surface.

(vi) **Excretion**: Specialised cells called **flame cells** help in osmoregulation and excretion.

(vii) **Reproduction:** Sexes are not separate. Fertilisation is **internal** and development is **indirect** through many larval stages.

(viii) **Regeneration:** Some members like *Planaria* possess high **regeneration** capacity.

Examples: *Taenia* (Tapeworm), *Fasciola* (liver fluke)

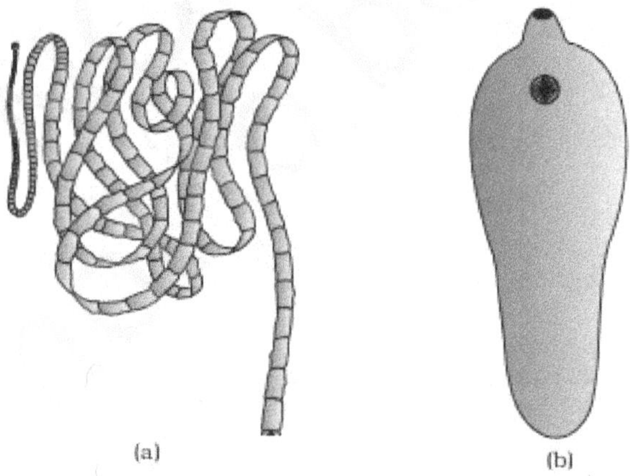

Fig. 9. a) Tape worm b) liver fluke

(v) Phylum – Aschelminthes

(i) **Habitat**: They may be freeliving, aquatic and terrestrial or parasitic in plants and animals. The body of the aschelminthes is **circular** in cross-section, hence, the name ***roundworms* (Fig.10)**.

(ii) **Symmetry:** Bilaterally symmetrical.

(iii) **Organisation:** Roundworms are **triploblastic** and **pseudocoelomate** and have **organ-system** level of body organisation.

(iv) **Alimentary canal** is complete with a well-developed **muscular pharynx.**

(v) **Excretion**: An excretory tube removes body wastes from the body cavity through the **excretory pore**.

(vi) **Reproduction**: Sexes are separate (**dioecious**), i.e., males and females are distinct. Often females are longer than males.

(vii) **Fertilisation** is internal and development may be **direct** (the young ones resemble the adult) or **indirect**.

Examples: *Ascaris* (Round Worm), *Wuchereria* (Filaria worm), *Ancylostoma* (Hookworm).

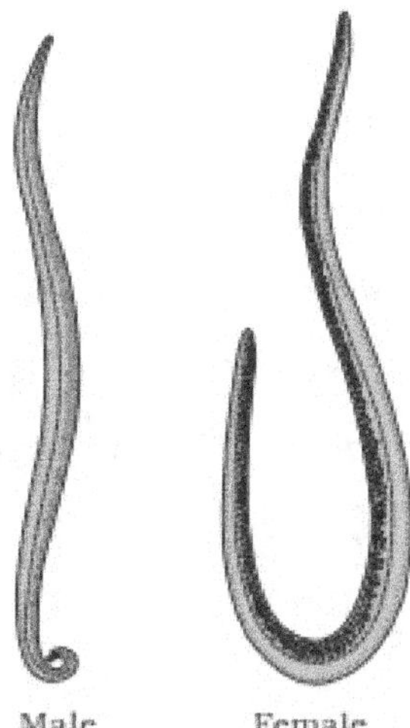

Fig 10. Roundworms

(VI) Phylum – Annelida

(i) **Habitat**: Aquatic (marine and fresh water) or terrestrial; free-living and sometimes parasitic. Their body surface is divided into **segments** or **metameres** and, hence, the phylum name Annelida (Latin, *annulus*: little ring) (**Fig.11**).

(ii) **Symmetry**: Bilateral symmetry.

(iii) **Organisation:** Exhibit organ-system level of body organisation and are triploblastic, metamerically segmented and **coelomate** animals.

(iv) **Locomotion**: Possess longitudinal and circular muscles which help in locomotion. Aquatic annelids like *Nereis* possess lateral appendages, **parapodia**, which help in swimming. **Circulatory system:** A **closed** circulatory system is present.

(v) **Excretion**: **Nephridia** (sing. nephridium) help in osmoregulation and excretion.

(vi) **Neural system** consists of paired **ganglia** (sing. ganglion) connected by lateral nerves to a double **ventral nerve cord**.

(vii) **Reproduction:** Reproduction is sexual. *Nereis,* an aquatic form, is **dioecious**, but earthworms and leeches are **monoecious**.

Examples: *Nereis, Pheretima* (Earthworm) and *Hirudinaria* (Blood sucking leech).

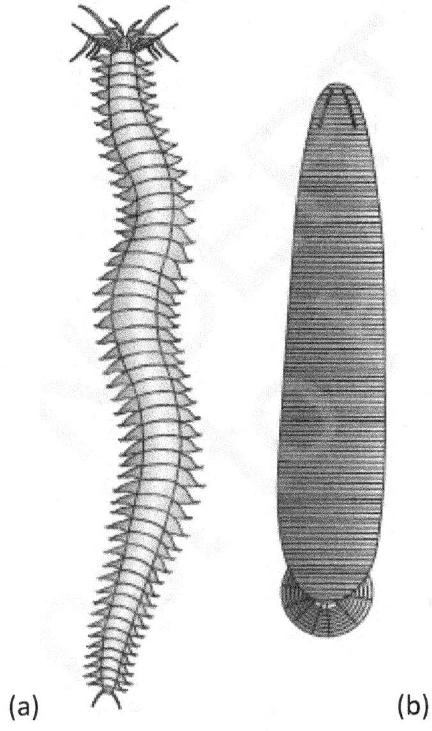

Fig 11. a) *Nereis* b) *Hirudinaria*

(VII) Phylum – Arthropoda

This is the **largest phylum** of Animalia which includes insects. Over two-thirds of all named species on earth are arthropods **(Fig.12)**.

(i) **Symmetry**: Bilaterally symmetrical, triploblastic, segmented and **coelomate** animals.

(ii) **Organisation:** They have organ-system level of organisation.

(iii) **Skeleton**: Body is covered by **chitinous** exoskeleton and consists of **head, thorax** and **abdomen.**

(iv) **Locomotion**: They have **jointed appendages (arthros**-joint, **poda**-appendages).

(v) **Respiratory organs** are gills, book gills, book lungs or tracheal system.

(vi) **Circulatory system** is of **open** type.

(vii) **Sensory organs** like antennae, eyes (compound and simple), statocysts or balance organs are present.

(viii) **Excretion** takes place through **malpighian tubules**.

(ix) **Reproduction:** They are mostly **dioecious**. **Fertilisation** is usually **internal**. They are mostly **oviparous**. **Development** may be **direct** or **indirect**.

Examples: Economically important insects – *Apis* (Honey bee), *Bombyx* (Silkworm), *Laccifer* (Lac insect)

Vectors – *Anopheles, Culex* and *Aedes* (Mosquitoes)

Gregarious pest – *Locusta* (Locust)

Living fossil – *Limulus* (King crab).

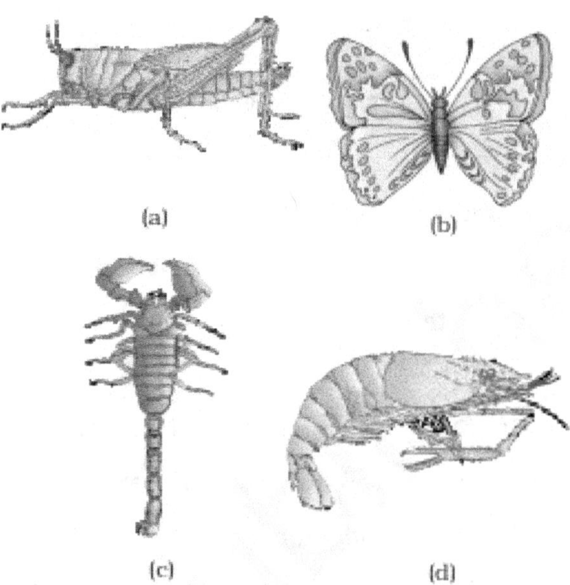

Fig 12. Arthropodes a) Locust b) butterfly c) scorpion d) prawn

(VIII) Phylum – Mollusca

(i) **Habitat**: **Molluscs** are terrestrial or aquatic (marine or fresh water) and represent the **second largest** animal phylum (**Fig.13**).

(ii) **Symmetry**: Bilaterally symmetrical, triploblastic and coelomate animals.

(iii) **Organisation:** They have organ-system level of organisation.

(iv) **Body** is covered by a calcareous shell and is unsegmented with a distinct **head, muscular foot** and **visceral hump.**

(v) **Mantle:** A soft and spongy layer of skin forms a **mantle** over the visceral hump.

(vi) **Respiratory and excretory structure**: The space between the hump and the mantle is called the **mantle cavity** in which feather like **gills** are present. They have respiratory and excretory functions.

(vii) **Sense organs:** The anterior head region has sensory **tentacles.**

(viii) **Radula**: The mouth contains a file-like rasping organ for feeding, called **radula.**

(ix) **Reproduction:** They are usually **dioecious** and **oviparous** with **indirect** development.

Examples: *Pila* (Apple snail), *Pinctada* (Pearl oyster), *Sepia* (Cuttlefish), *Loligo* (Squid), *Octopus* (Devil fish), *Aplysia* (Seahare), *Dentalium* (Tusk shell) and *Chaetopleura* (Chiton).

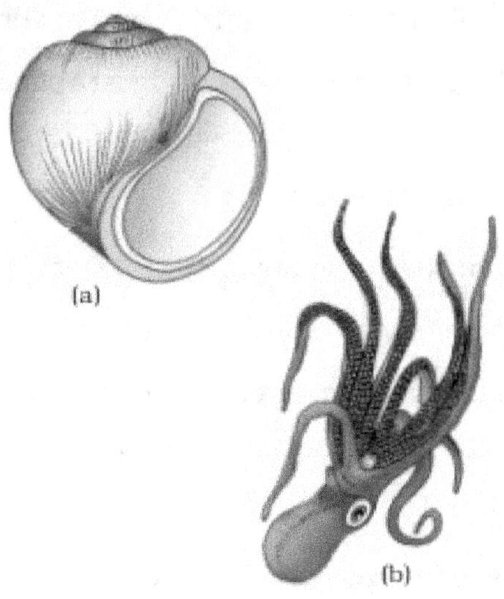

Fig.13. Mollusca a) *Pila* b) Octopus

(IX) Phylum – Echinodermata (Spiny bodied animals).

These animals have an endoskeleton of calcareous **ossicles** and, hence, the name Echinodermata (Spiny bodied) (**Fig.14**).

    (i)   **Habitat**: All are **marine**.

    (ii) **Symmetry**: Adults are **radially** symmetrical but larvae are **bilaterally** symmetrical.

    (iii) **Organisation:** They have organ-system level of organization and are triploblastic and coelomate animals.

    (iv) **Digestive system** is complete with mouth on the **lower** (ventral) side and anus on the upper (dorsal) side.

    (v) **Water vascular system:** The most distinctive feature of echinoderms is the presence of **water vascular system** which helps in **locomotion,** capture and transport of **food** and **respiration.**

    (vi) **Excretory system** is absent.

(vii) **Reproduction:** Sexes are separate. Reproduction is sexual. Fertilisation is usually **external**. Development is **indirect** with free-swimming larva (**bipinnaria, doliolaria**).

Examples: *Asterias* (Star fish), *Echinus* (Sea urchin), *Antedon* (Sea lily), *Cucumaria* (Sea cucumber) and *Ophiura* (Brittle star).

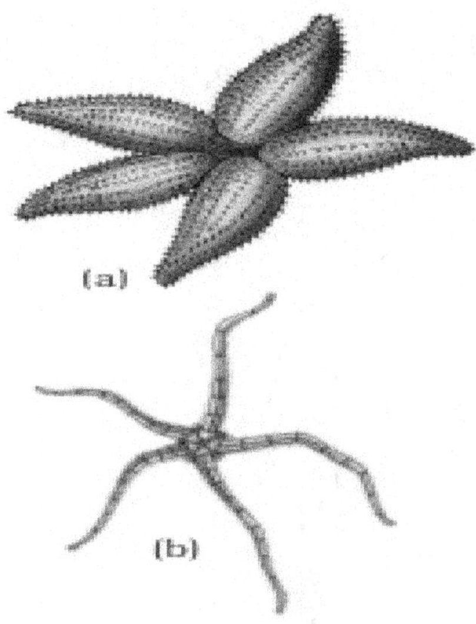

Fig. 14. Echinodermata a) *Asterias* b) *Ophiura*

(X) Phylum – Hemichordata

Hemichordata was earlier considered as a sub-phylum under phylum Chordata. But now it is placed as a separate phylum under non-chordata. Hemichordata have a rudimentary structure in the collar region called stomochord, a structure similar to notochord. The salient features of phylum are as follows:

i) This phylum consists of a small group of **worm-like** marine animals with organ-system level of organisation.

ii) They are bilaterally symmetrical, triploblastic and coelomate animals.

iii) The body is cylindrical and is composed of an anterior **proboscis**, a **collar** and a long **trunk (Fig.15)**.

iv) Circulatory system is of **open** type. Respiration takes place through **gills**. Excretory organ is **proboscis gland**.

v) Sexes are separate. Fertilisation is external. Development is indirect (**tornaria** larva).

Examples: *Balanoglossus* and *Saccoglossus.*

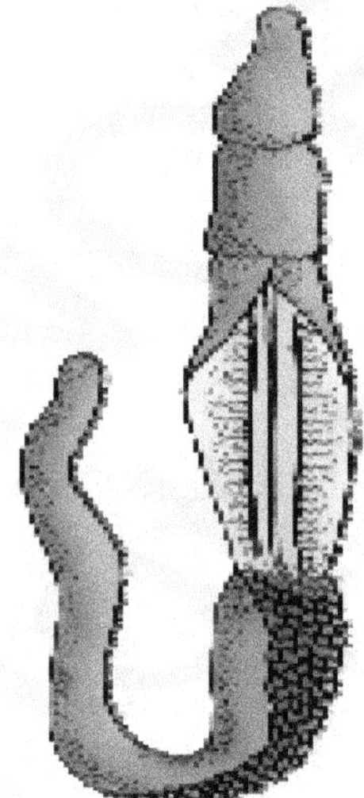

Fig. 15. *Balanoglossus*

(XI) Phylum – Chordata

Animals belonging to phylum Chordata are fundamentally characterised by the presence of a ***notochord***, a ***dorsal hollow nerve cord*** and ***paired pharyngeal gill slits*** (***Fig.16***). These are bilaterally symmetrical, triploblastic, coelomate with organ-system level of organisation. They possess a post anal tail and a closed circulatory system.

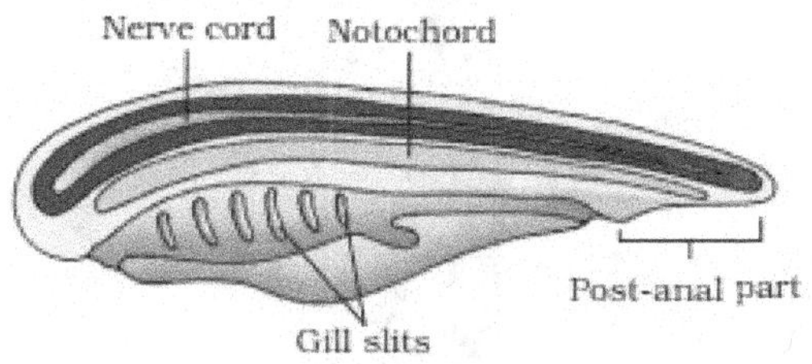

Fig. 16. Chordata characteristics

Table 1: Comparison of salient features of chordates and non-chordates.

S.No.	Chordates	Non-chordates
1.	Notochord present.	Notochord absent.
2.	Central nervous system is dorsal, hollow and single.	Central nervous system is ventral, solid and double.
3.	Pharynx perforated by gill slits.	Gill slits are absent.
4.	Heart is ventral.	Heart is dorsal (if present).
5.	A post-anal part (tail) is present.	Post-anal tail is absent.

Phylum **Chordata** is divided into three subphyla:

i)   ***Urochordata*** or ***Tunicata***: In Urochordata, notochord is present only in larval tail. Examples: *Ascidia*, *Salpa*, *Doliolum* (**Fig.**17).

ii)   ***Cephalochordata:*** In Cephalochordate, notochord extends from head to tail region and is persistent throughout their life. Example *Branchiostoma* (Amphioxus or Lancelet).

Subphyla Urochordata and Cephalochordata are often referred to as ***protochordates*** and are exclusively marine.

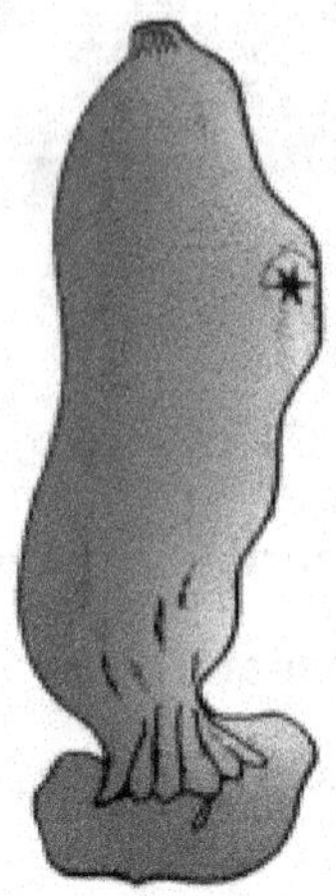

Fig 17. *Ascidia*

iii) Vertebrata. The members of subphylum Vertebrata possess **notochord** during the embryonic period. The notochord is replaced by a cartilaginous or bony **vertebral column** in the adult. ***Thus all vertebrates are chordates but all chordates are not vertebrates***. Besides the basic chordate characters, vertebrates have a ventral muscular heart with two, three or four chambers, kidneys for excretion and osmoregulation and paired appendages which may be fins or limbs.

The subphylum **vertebrata** is divided as follows:

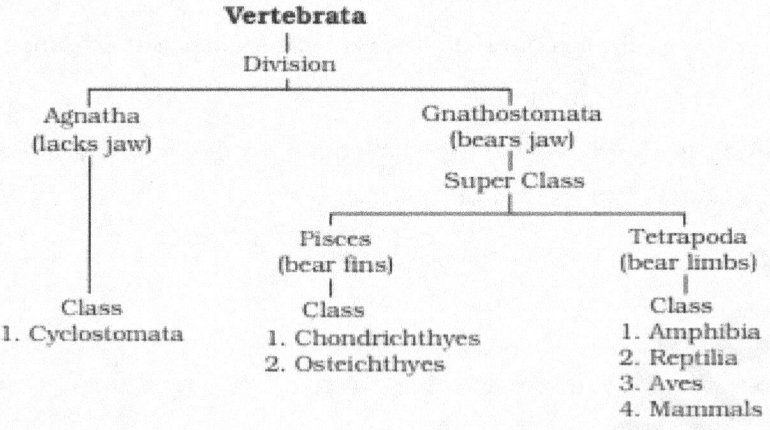

i) All living members of the class Cyclostomata are **ectoparasites** on some fishes.

ii) They have an elongated body bearing 6-15 pairs of *gill slits* for respiration.

iii) They have a sucking and **circular** mouth without jaws (*Fig.*18).

iv) Their body is devoid of scales and paired fins.

v) Cranium and vertebral column are **cartilaginous**.

vi) Circulation is of closed type. Cyclostomes are marine but migrate for spawning to fresh water. After spawning, within a few days, they die. Their larvae, after metamorphosis, return to the ocean.

Examples: *Petromyzon* (Lamprey) and *Myxine* (Hagfish).

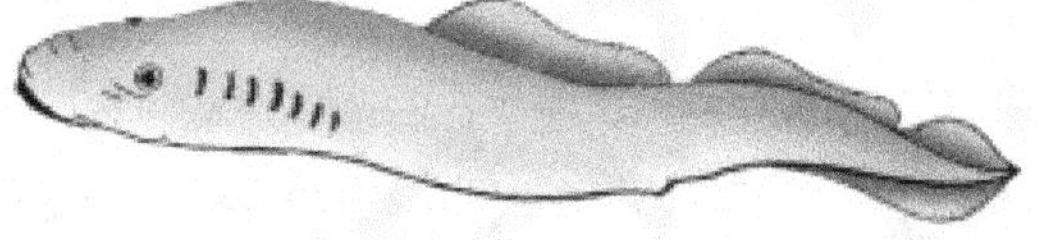

Fig 18. *Petromyzon*

i)They are marine animals with streamlined body and have **cartilaginous endoskeleton** (*Fig.*19).

ii) Mouth is located ventrally.

iii) **Notochord** is **persistent** throughout life.

iv) Gill slits are separate and without *operculum* (gill cover).

v) The skin is tough, containing minute *placoid scales*.

vi) Teeth are modified placoid scales which are backwardly directed. Their jaws are very powerful. These animals are predaceous.

vii) Due to the absence of **air bladder**, they have to swim constantly to avoid sinking.

viii) Heart is two-chambered (one auricle and one ventricle).

ix) Some of them have **electric organs** (e.g., *Torpedo*) and some possess **poison sting** (e.g., *Trygon*).

x) They are cold-blooded (**poikilothermous**) animals, i.e., they lack the capacity to regulate their body temperature.

xi) Sexes are separate. In males pelvic fins bear claspers. They have internal fertilisation and many of them are **viviparous**.

Examples: *Scoliodon* (Dog fish), *Pristis* (Saw fish), *Carcharodon* (Great white shark), *Trygon* (Sting ray).

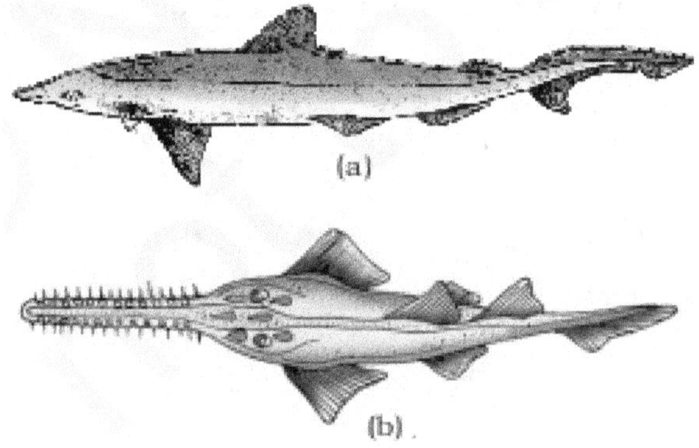

Fig. 19. Cartilaginous fishes a) *Scoliodon* b) *Pristis*

(iii) Class – Osteichthyes

i) Osteichthyes includes both marine and fresh water fishes with **bony endoskeleton**.

ii) Their body is streamlined. Mouth is mostly **terminal** (**Fig.**20).

iii) They have **four pairs** of gills which are covered by an **operculum** on each side.

iii) Skin is covered with cycloid/ctenoid scales. **Air bladder** is present which regulates buoyancy.

iv) Heart is two chambered (one auricle and one ventricle).

v)They are cold-blooded animals.

vi) Sexes are separate. Fertilisation is usually external. They are mostly oviparous and development is direct.

Examples: **Marine** – *Exocoetus* (Flying fish), *Hippocampus* (Sea horse);

Freshwater – *Labeo* (Rohu), *Catla* (Katla), *Clarias* (Magur);

Aquarium – *Betta* (Fighting fish), *Pterophyllum* (Angel fish).

Fig. 20. a) *Hippocampus* b) *Catla*

(iv) Class – Amphibia

i)As the name indicates (*Gr., Amphi* : dual, *bios*, life), amphibians can live in aquatic as well as terrestrial habitats (**Fig.21**). Water is must for the completion of their life cycle, as fertilization occurs in water.

ii) Most of them have two pairs of limbs. Body is divisible into **head** and **trunk**. Tail may be present in some.

iii) The amphibian skin is moist (without scales).

iv)The eyes have eyelids. A **tympanum** represents the ear.

v) Alimentary canal, urinary and reproductive tracts open into a common chamber called ***cloaca*** which opens to the exterior by cloacal aperture.

vi) **Respiration** is by gills, lungs and through skin.

vii) The heart is three chambered (two auricles and one ventricle). These are cold-blooded animals.

viii) Sexes are separate. Fertilisation is external. They are oviparous and development is indirect (tadpole larva).

Examples: *Bufo* (Toad), *Rana* (Frog), *Hyla* (Tree frog), *Salamandra* (Salamander), *Ichthyophis* (Limbless amphibia).

Fig. 21. Amphibia a) *Salamandra* b) *Rana*

(v) Class – Reptilia

i) The class name refers to their creeping or crawling mode of locomotion (*Latin, repere* or *reptum*, to creep or crawl). They are mostly terrestrial animals and their body is covered by dry and cornified skin, epidermal ***scales*** or ***scutes*** (**Fig.22**).

ii) They do not have external ear openings. Tympanum represents ear.

iii) Limbs, when present, are two pairs.

iv) Heart is usually three-chambered, but **four-chambered in crocodiles**.

v) Reptiles are poikilotherms.

vi) Snakes and lizards shed their scales as skin cast.

vii) Sexes are separate. Fertilisation is internal. They are **oviparous** and development is direct.

Examples: *Chelone* (Turtle), *Testudo* (Tortoise), *Chameleon* (Tree lizard), *Calotes* (Garden lizard), *Crocodilus* (Crocodile), *Alligator* (Alligator). *Hemidactylus* (Wall lizard), **Poisonous snakes** – *Naja* (Cobra), *Bangarus* (Krait), *Vipera* (Viper).

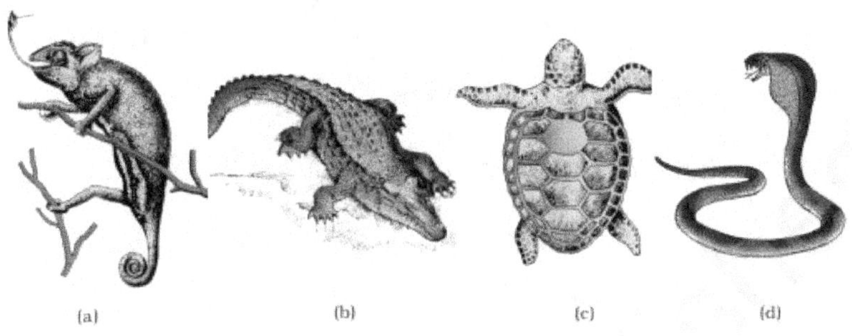

Fig.22. Reptiles: a) *Chameleon*, b) *Crocodilus* , c) *Chelone* , d) *Naja*

(vi) Class – Aves

i)The characteristic features of Aves (birds) are the presence of *feathers* and most of them can fly except flightless birds (e.g., Ostrich).

ii)They possess *beak* (*Fig.*23). The forelimbs are modified into *wings*. The hind limbs generally have scales and are modified for walking, swimming or clasping the tree branches.

iii) Skin is dry without glands except the **oil gland** at the base of the tail.

iv) Endoskeleton is fully ossified (**bony**) and the long bones are hollow with *air cavities* (pneumatic).

v) The digestive tract of birds has additional chambers, the **crop** and **gizzard**.

vi) Heart is completely **four chambered**. They are warm-blooded (*homoiothermous*) animals, i.e., they are able to maintain a constant body temperature.

vii)Respiration is by lungs. Air sacs connected to lungs supplement respiration.

viii) Sexes are separate. Fertilisation is internal. They are oviparous and development is direct.

Examples: *Corvus* (Crow), *Columba* (Pigeon), *Psittacula* (Parrot), *Struthio* (Ostrich), *Pavo* (Peacock), *Aptenodytes* (Penguin), *Neophron* (Vulture).

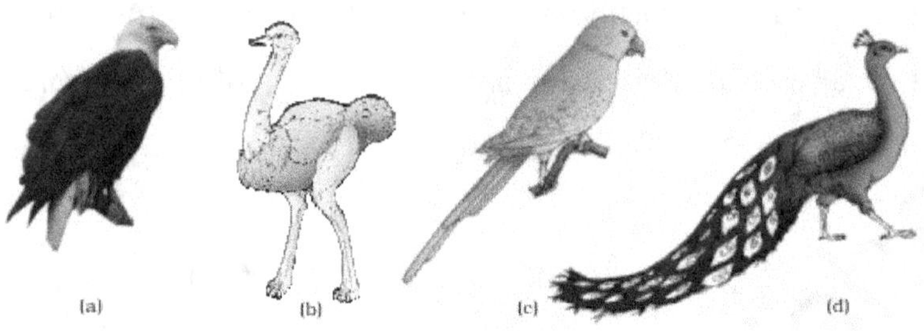

Fig. 23.Birds a) *Neophron*, b) *Struthio*, c) *Psittacula*, d) *Pavo*

(vii) Class – Mammalia

i)They are found in a variety of habitats – polar ice caps, deserts, mountains, forests, grasslands and dark caves. Some of them have adapted to fly or live in water.

ii) The most unique mammalian characteristic is the presence of milk producing glands (***mammary glands***) by which the young ones are nourished.

iii) They have two pairs of limbs, adapted for walking, running, climbing, burrowing, swimming or flying (**Fig.24**).

iv) The skin of mammals is unique in possessing ***hair***. External ears or ***pinnae*** are present.

v) Different types of teeth are present in the jaw.

vi) Heart is four chambered. They are homoiothermous.

vi) Respiration is by lungs.

vii) Sexes are separate and fertilisation is internal. They are viviparous with few exceptions and development is direct.

Examples: **Oviparous**-*Ornithorhynchus* (Platypus); **Viviparous** - *Macropus* (Kangaroo), *Pteropus* (Flying fox), *Camelus* (Camel), *Macaca* (Monkey), *Rattus* (Rat), *Canis* (Dog), *Felis* (Cat), *Elephas* (Elephant), *Equus* (Horse), *Delphinus* (Common dolphin), *Balaenoptera* (Blue whale), *Panthera tigris* (Tiger), *Panthera leo* (Lion).

Fig. 24. Mammals a) *Ornithorhynchus,* b) *Macropus,* c) *Pteropus,* d) *Balaenoptera*